Percentages Book

by Jerry Pallotta
Illustrated by Rob Bolster

Cartwheel
·B·O·O·K·S· ®
SCHOLASTIC INC.

New York   Toronto   London   Auckland   Sydney   Mexico City   New Delhi   Hong Kong

Thank you to Andy Pallotta who is twenty-five percent of my brothers.
He is also sixteen point sixty-six percent of my brothers and sisters.

—— *Jerry Pallotta*

This book is dedicated to my art teacher, Tom DelSignore. He always made the art room a fun place to be.

—— *Rob Bolster*

This really happened, but no one believes me. On the day our class was going to learn percentages, I noticed a lot of candy on my teacher's desk. I wondered what percentage each of us would get. Then a mini-spaceship started talking. . . .

Earthlings, we have come to visit your planet. If you give us TWIZZLERS® Twists, we will teach you about percentages.

$$\frac{75}{100} = .75 = 75\%$$

FRACTION   DECIMAL   PERCENTAGE

These three equal numbers identify parts of a whole amount.

. . . and here are some math symbols to help you figure out percentages.

÷ This is a division sign. It is used to divide numbers. A fraction is a numerator divided by a denominator. The line between a numerator and a denominator is called a fraction bar and is also considered a division sign.

This is a decimal point. ●
It is used to separate whole numbers from decimals.

% This is a percentage symbol. It is used to show that a number is a percentage of something. We use percentages in everyday life.

This is an equal sign. It is used to show that two or more numbers are equal in value.

This is a multiplication sign or a times sign. Multiplication is important. To change a decimal to a percentage, you multiply by one hundred.

These candies are called TWIZZLERS Twists.

STRAWBERRY TWIST

LICORICE TWIST

These are our mini-spaceships.
Do not be afraid. We are here to help you.

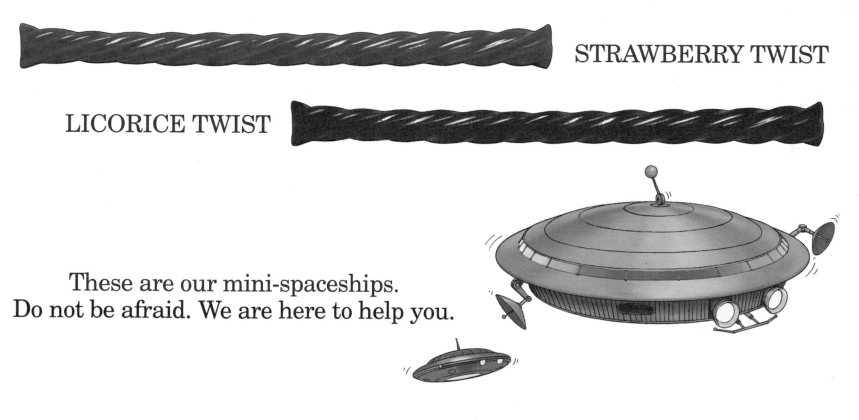

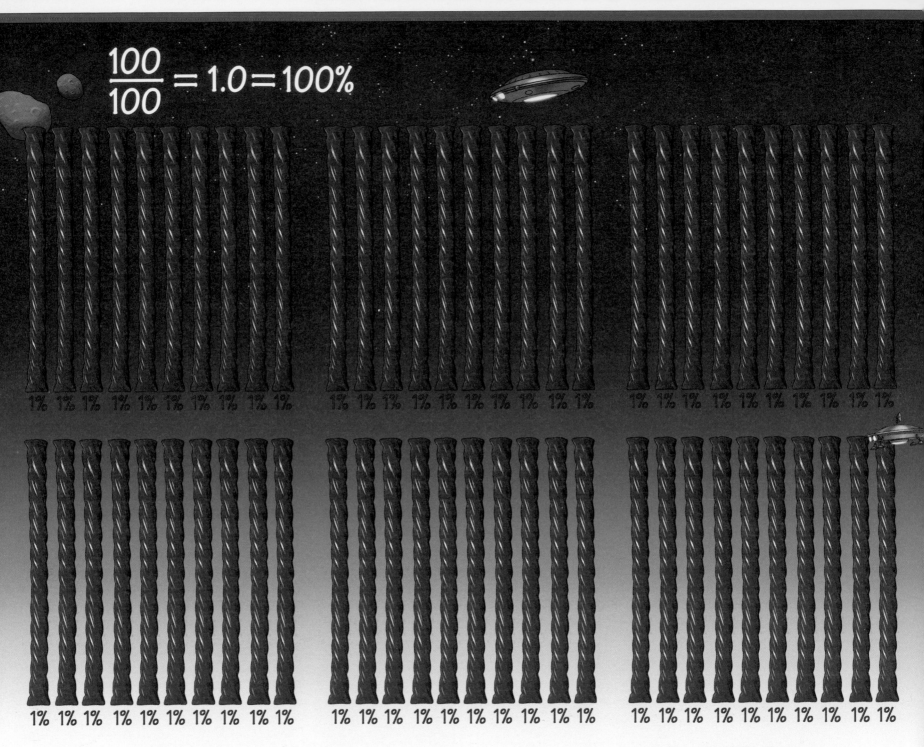

$$\frac{100}{100} = 1.0 = 100\%$$

1% 1% 1% 1% 1% 1% 1% 1% 1% 1%   1% 1% 1% 1% 1% 1% 1% 1% 1% 1%   1% 1% 1% 1% 1% 1% 1% 1% 1% 1%

1% 1% 1% 1% 1% 1% 1% 1% 1% 1%   1% 1% 1% 1% 1% 1% 1% 1% 1% 1%   1% 1% 1% 1% 1% 1% 1% 1% 1% 1%

On this page and the next page are one hundred TWIZZLERS Twists.
Percent means "per hundred." One hundred percent is the whole group.

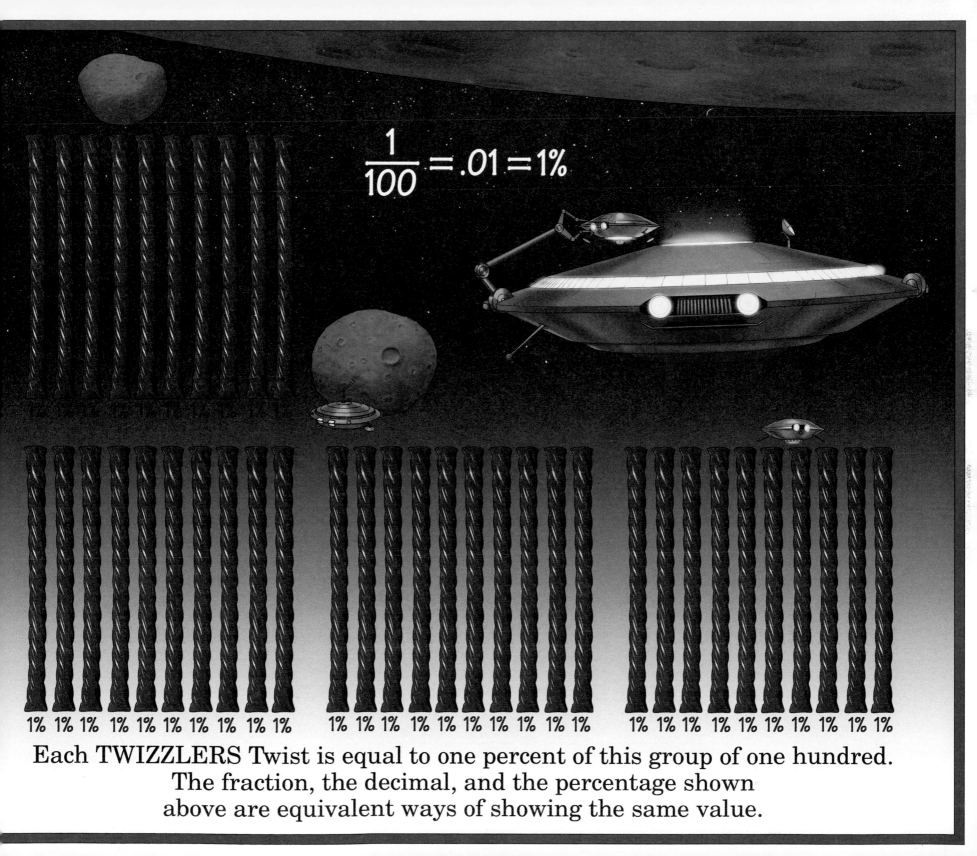

$$\frac{1}{100} = .01 = 1\%$$

1% 1% 1% 1% 1% 1% 1% 1% 1% 1%   1% 1% 1% 1% 1% 1% 1% 1% 1% 1%   1% 1% 1% 1% 1% 1% 1% 1% 1% 1%

Each TWIZZLERS Twist is equal to one percent of this group of one hundred.
The fraction, the decimal, and the percentage shown
above are equivalent ways of showing the same value.

1 2 3 4 5 6 7 8 9 0

BASE 10

There are hundreds of different alphabets in the galaxy, but almost everyone uses the same number system. You can write any number with the symbols zero, one, two, three, four, five, six, seven, eight, and nine. After nine comes ten, which is really one group of ten and zero ones. It is a base-ten system. Aliens from other planets probably use the same base-ten system.

23.86

It is important to learn place value. Here is a number we picked at random. Twenty-three point eighty-six. This number has two tens, three ones, a decimal point, eight tenths, and six hundredths. The position, or place of a number in relation to the decimal point, determines its place value.

PLACE VALUE

millions hundred thousands ten thousands thousands hundreds tens ones tenths hundredths thousandths

1,864,527.309

whole numbers

decimals

decimal point

Wow! Here is a big number. One million eight hundred sixty-four thousand five hundred twenty-seven point three zero nine.

$$\frac{90}{100} = .9 = 90\%$$

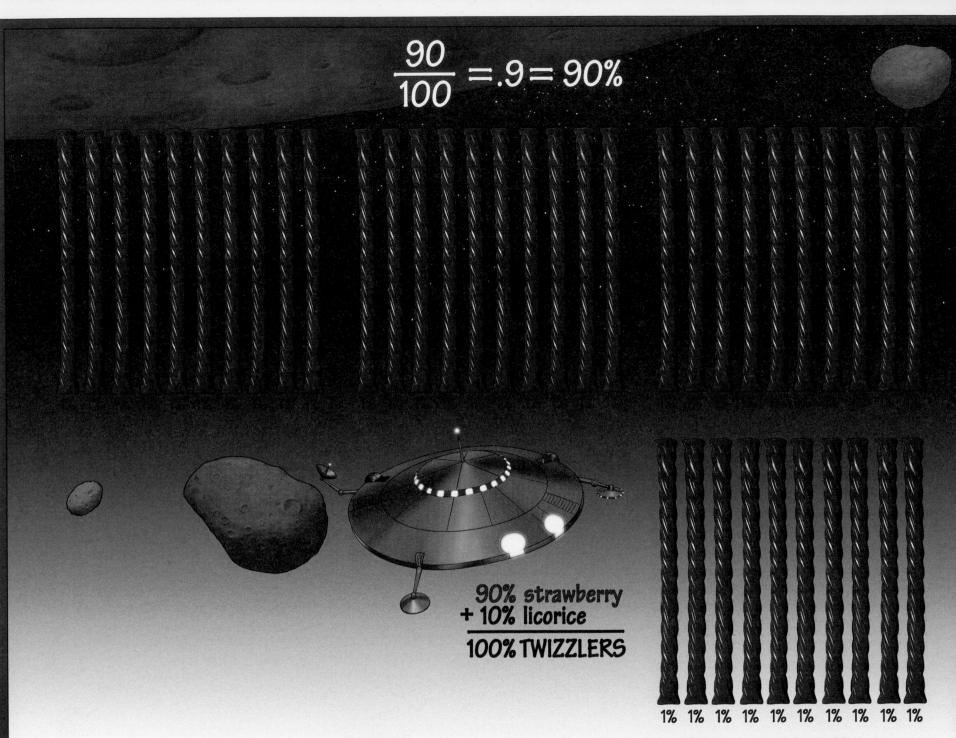

90% strawberry
+ 10% licorice
—————————
100% TWIZZLERS

1% 1% 1% 1% 1% 1% 1% 1% 1% 1%

Earthlings, notice the difference on these two pages. There are still one hundred TWIZZLERS Twists, but only ninety of them are strawberry-flavored. Ten are licorice-flavored.

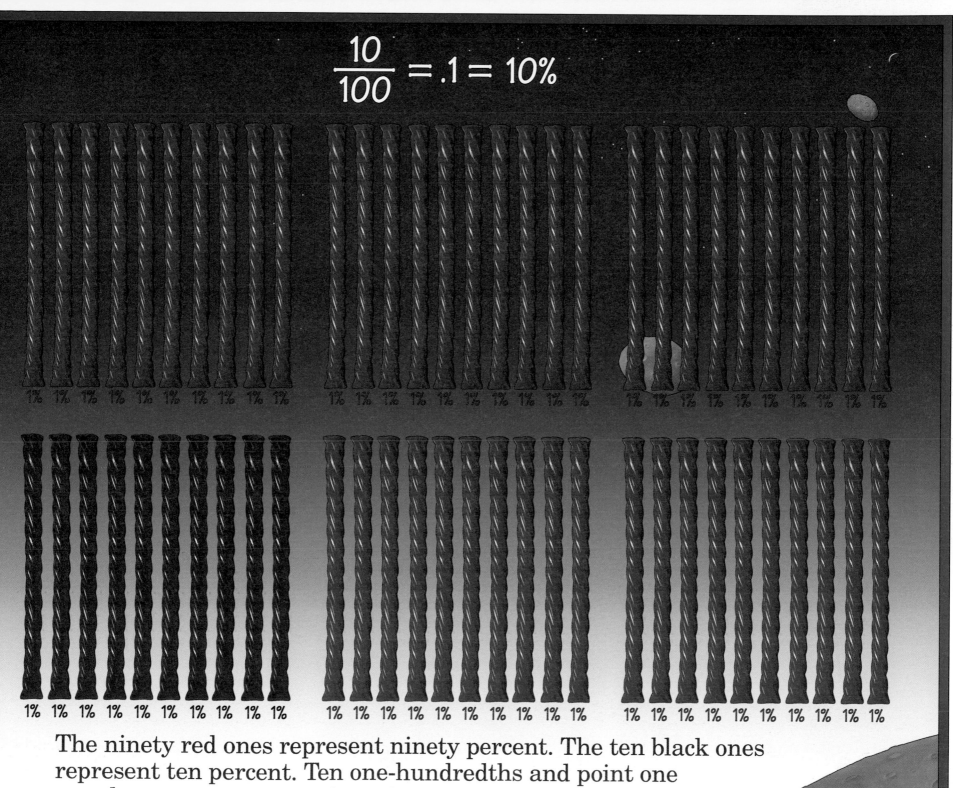

$$\frac{10}{100} = .1 = 10\%$$

The ninety red ones represent ninety percent. The ten black ones represent ten percent. Ten one-hundredths and point one are also correct ways to show this amount of licorice.

fraction		decimal		percentage
$\dfrac{1}{100}$	=	.01	=	1%
$\dfrac{2}{100}$	=	.02	=	2%
$\dfrac{3}{100}$	=	.03	=	3%
$\dfrac{4}{100}$	=	.04	=	4%
$\dfrac{5}{100}$	=	.05	=	5%
$\dfrac{6}{100}$	=	.06	=	6%
$\dfrac{7}{100}$	=	.07	=	7%
$\dfrac{8}{100}$	=	.08	=	8%
$\dfrac{9}{100}$	=	.09	=	9%
$\dfrac{10}{100}$	=	.1	=	10%

fraction		simplified fraction		decimal		percentage
$\dfrac{10}{100}$	=	$\dfrac{1}{10}$	=	.1	=	10%
$\dfrac{20}{100}$	=	$\dfrac{2}{10}$	=	.2	=	20%
$\dfrac{30}{100}$	=	$\dfrac{3}{10}$	=	.3	=	30%
$\dfrac{40}{100}$	=	$\dfrac{4}{10}$	=	.4	=	40%
$\dfrac{50}{100}$	=	$\dfrac{5}{10}$	=	.5	=	50%
$\dfrac{60}{100}$	=	$\dfrac{6}{10}$	=	.6	=	60%
$\dfrac{70}{100}$	=	$\dfrac{7}{10}$	=	.7	=	70%
$\dfrac{80}{100}$	=	$\dfrac{8}{10}$	=	.8	=	80%
$\dfrac{90}{100}$	=	$\dfrac{9}{10}$	=	.9	=	90%
$\dfrac{100}{100}$	=	$\dfrac{10}{10}$	=	1.0	=	100%

Okay! You get the idea. Do you see any patterns?

Earthlings, here is how to figure out a percentage. Divide the top number of a fraction, the numerator, by the bottom number, the denominator. This will give you a decimal. Move the decimal point two places to the right. Drop the decimal point and add a percent sign.

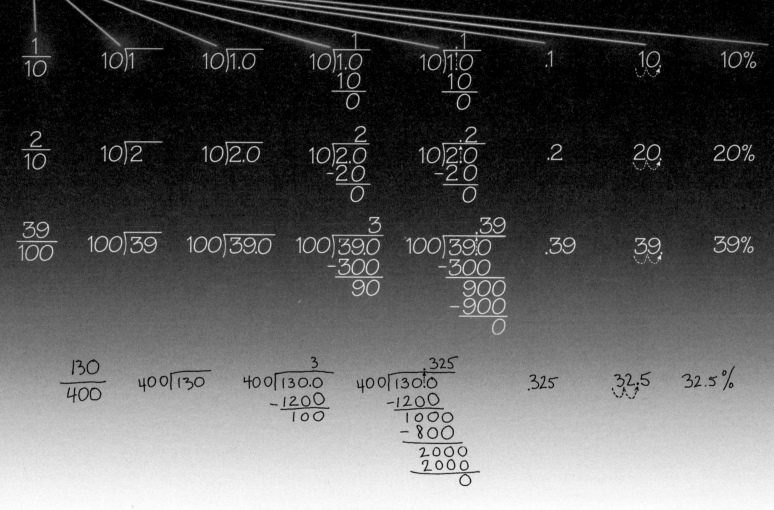

Try a difficult one.
Don't forget to show your work!

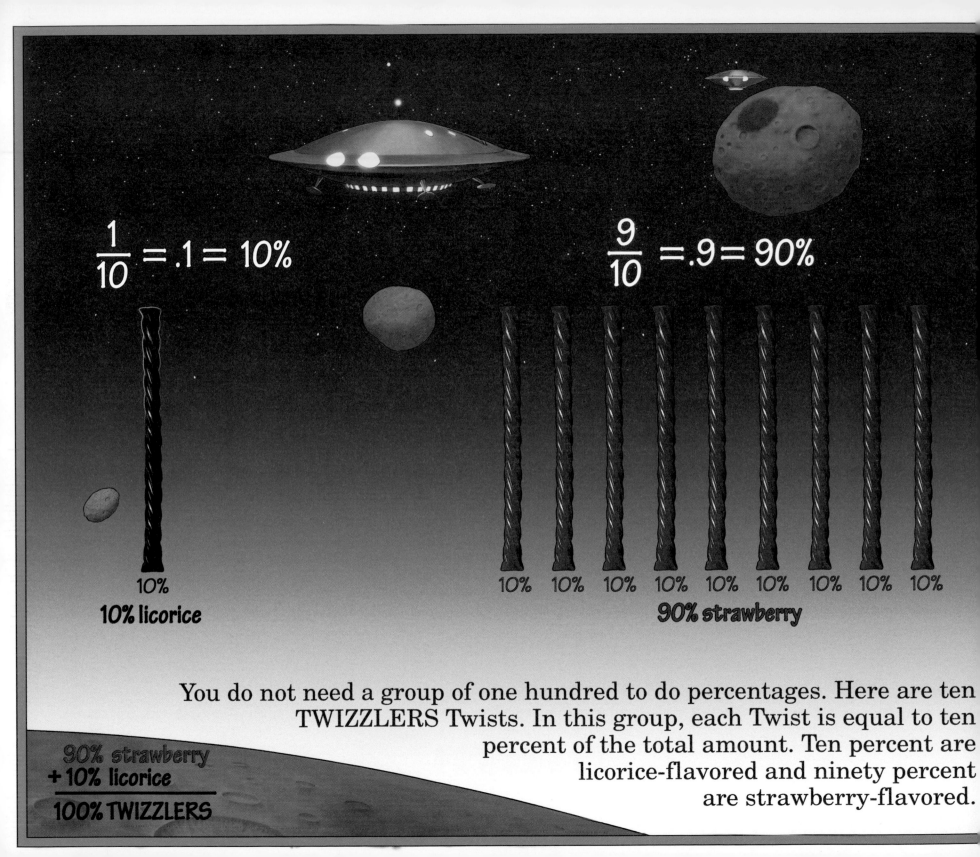

$$\frac{1}{10} = .1 = 10\%$$

$$\frac{9}{10} = .9 = 90\%$$

10%

10% licorice

10% 10% 10% 10% 10% 10% 10% 10% 10%

90% strawberry

You do not need a group of one hundred to do percentages. Here are ten TWIZZLERS Twists. In this group, each Twist is equal to ten percent of the total amount. Ten percent are licorice-flavored and ninety percent are strawberry-flavored.

90% strawberry
+ 10% licorice
――――――――――
100% TWIZZLERS

$$\frac{8}{10} = .8 = 80\%$$

$$\frac{2}{10} = .2 = 20\%$$

10% 10% 10% 10% 10% 10% 10% 10%

80% licorice

10% 10%

20% strawberry

20% strawberry
+80% licorice
_____
100% TWIZZLERS

Here is another group of ten TWIZZLERS Twists. Flavors and colors can
change but the math stays the same. Each piece is equal to ten percent.
Eighty percent are black and twenty percent are red.

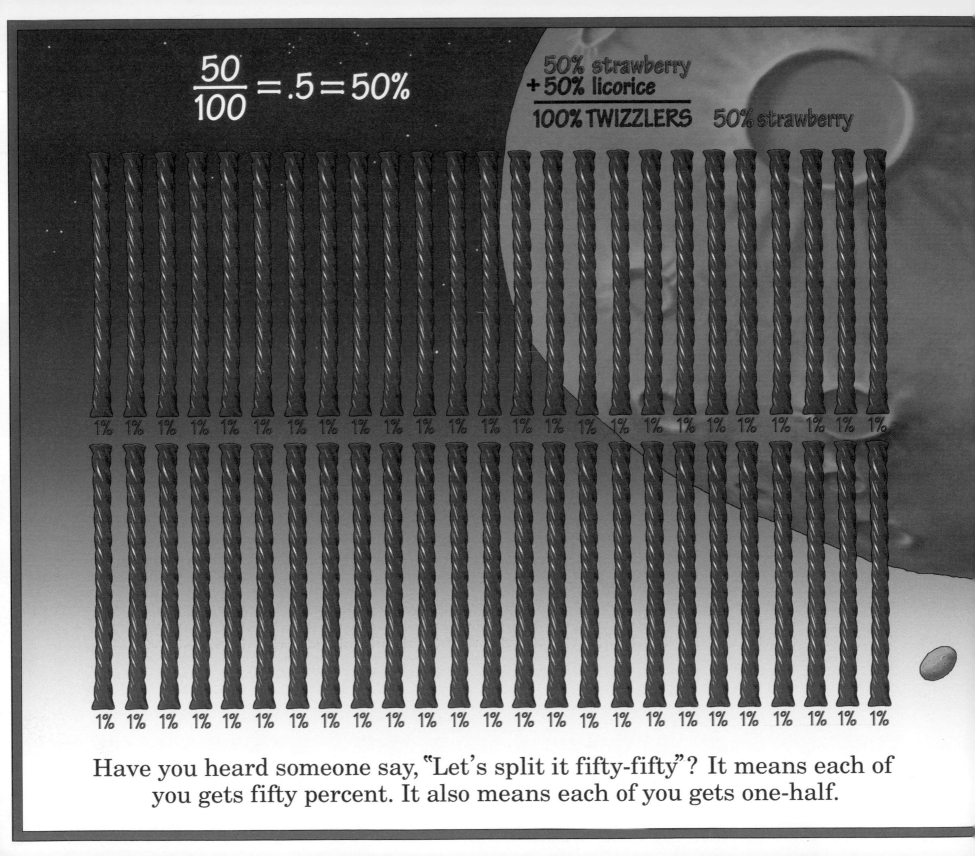

$$\frac{50}{100} = .5 = 50\%$$

$$\frac{50\% \text{ strawberry} + 50\% \text{ licorice}}{100\% \text{ TWIZZLERS}} \quad 50\% \text{ strawberry}$$

1% 1% 1% 1% 1% 1% 1% 1% 1% 1% 1% 1% 1% 1% 1% 1% 1% 1% 1% 1% 1% 1% 1% 1% 1%

1% 1% 1% 1% 1% 1% 1% 1% 1% 1% 1% 1% 1% 1% 1% 1% 1% 1% 1% 1% 1% 1% 1% 1% 1%

Have you heard someone say, "Let's split it fifty-fifty"? It means each of you gets fifty percent. It also means each of you gets one-half.

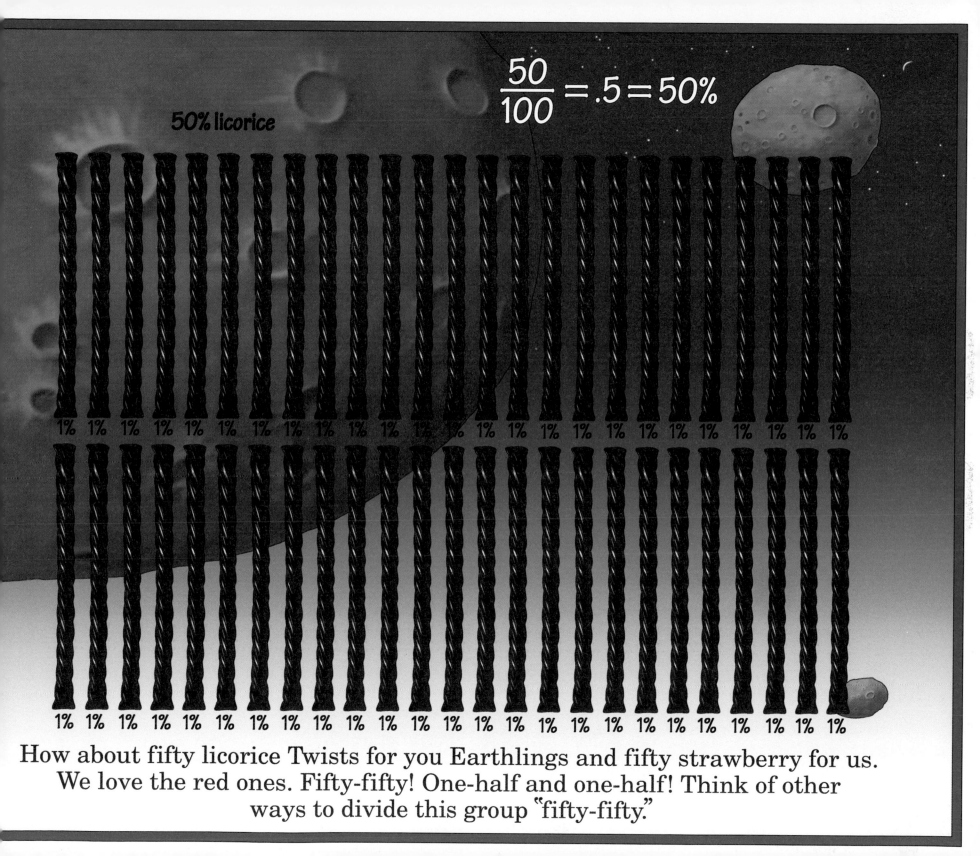

$$\frac{50}{100} = .5 = 50\%$$

50% licorice

1% 1% 1% 1% 1% 1% 1% 1% 1% 1% 1% 1% 1% 1% 1% 1% 1% 1% 1% 1% 1% 1% 1% 1% 1%

1% 1% 1% 1% 1% 1% 1% 1% 1% 1% 1% 1% 1% 1% 1% 1% 1% 1% 1% 1% 1% 1% 1% 1% 1%

How about fifty licorice Twists for you Earthlings and fifty strawberry for us. We love the red ones. Fifty-fifty! One-half and one-half! Think of other ways to divide this group "fifty-fifty."

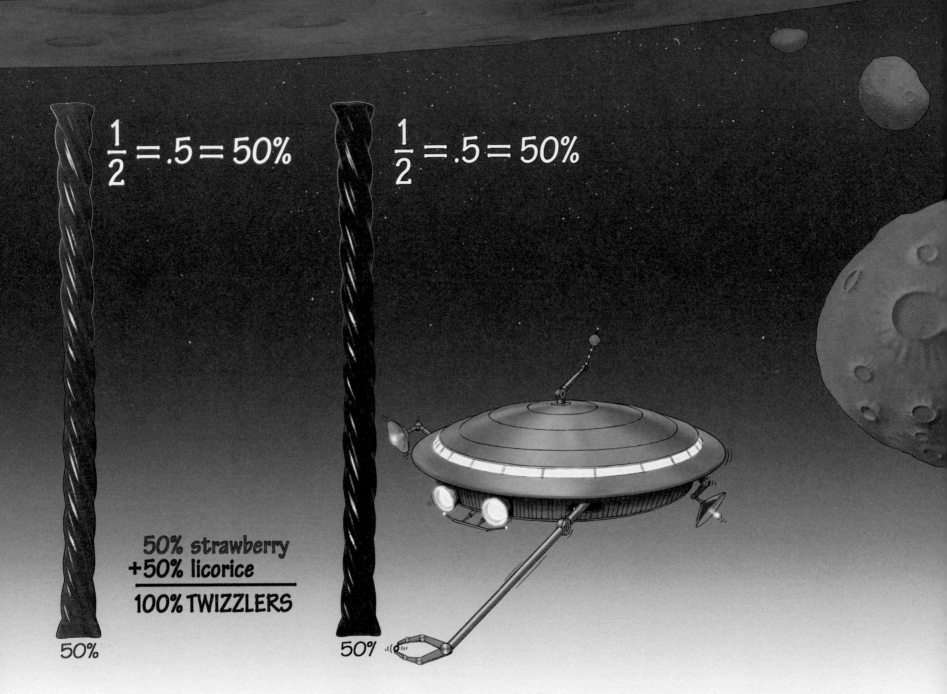

$\frac{1}{2} = .5 = 50\%$ $\frac{1}{2} = .5 = 50\%$

50% strawberry
+50% licorice
———————
100% TWIZZLERS

50%   50%

If there are only two TWIZZLERS Twists, each Twist is fifty percent of the total amount on this page. You can always figure out "fifty-fifty" by dividing by two. What is your favorite flavor?

$$\frac{1}{1} = 1.0 = 100\%$$

100%

Zap! Here is one TWIZZLERS Twist. It is one hundred percent of all the candy on this page. You would have to bite the Twist to get a smaller percentage than one hundred percent. Maybe a laser will help.

I'm glad we are learning percentages. Yesterday while walking to school, some of my classmates found ten thousand dollars on the street! Wow!

The police said our class could keep eight percent of the money as a reward. $10,000. × .08 = $800. Eight cents out of every dollar.

The principal of our school hoped we would keep nine percent. $10,000. × .09 = $900. Nine cents per dollar.

The insurance company approved a payment to our class for ten percent. $10,000. × .1 = $1,000. Ten cents per dollar.

The judge at the local courthouse ruled we could keep twelve percent. $10,000. × .12 = $1,200. Twelve cents per dollar.

But luckily the owners of the money came forward. They thanked our class, and we were rewarded with fifteen percent. Yeah! $10,000. × .15 = $1,500. Fifteen cents per dollar.

$$\frac{49}{50} = .98 = 98\% \qquad \frac{1}{50} = .02 = 2\%$$

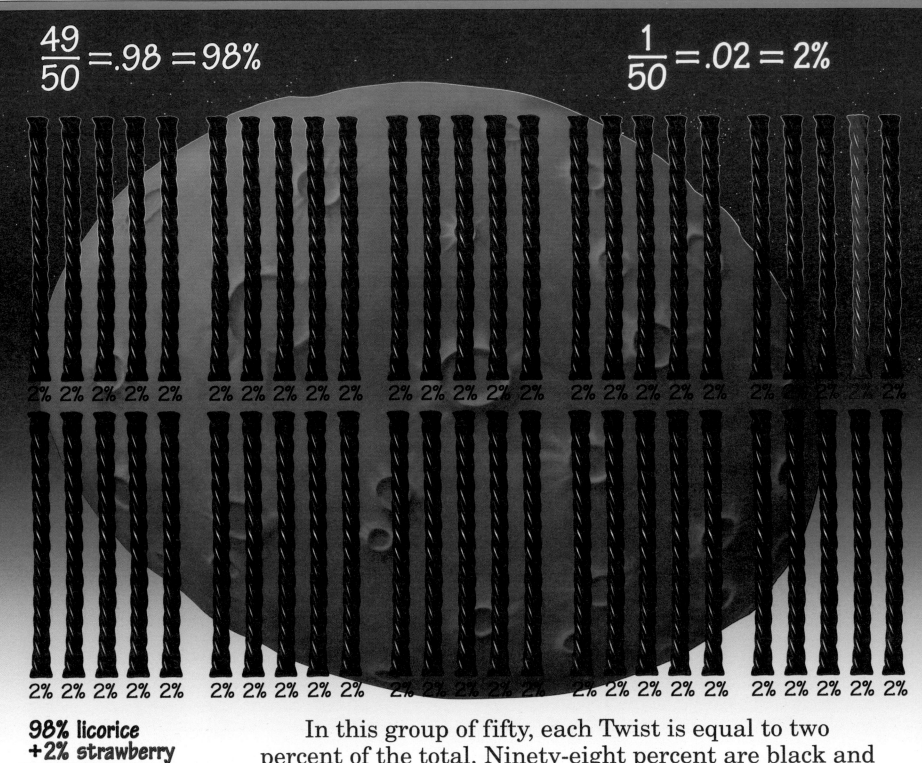

2% 2% 2% 2% 2% 2% 2% 2% 2% 2% 2% 2% 2% 2% 2% 2% 2% 2% 2% 2% 2% 2% 2% 2% 2%

2% 2% 2% 2% 2% 2% 2% 2% 2% 2% 2% 2% 2% 2% 2% 2% 2% 2% 2% 2% 2% 2% 2% 2% 2%

98% licorice
+2% strawberry
100% TWIZZLERS

In this group of fifty, each Twist is equal to two percent of the total. Ninety-eight percent are black and two percent are red. Watch out for meteors and asteroids.

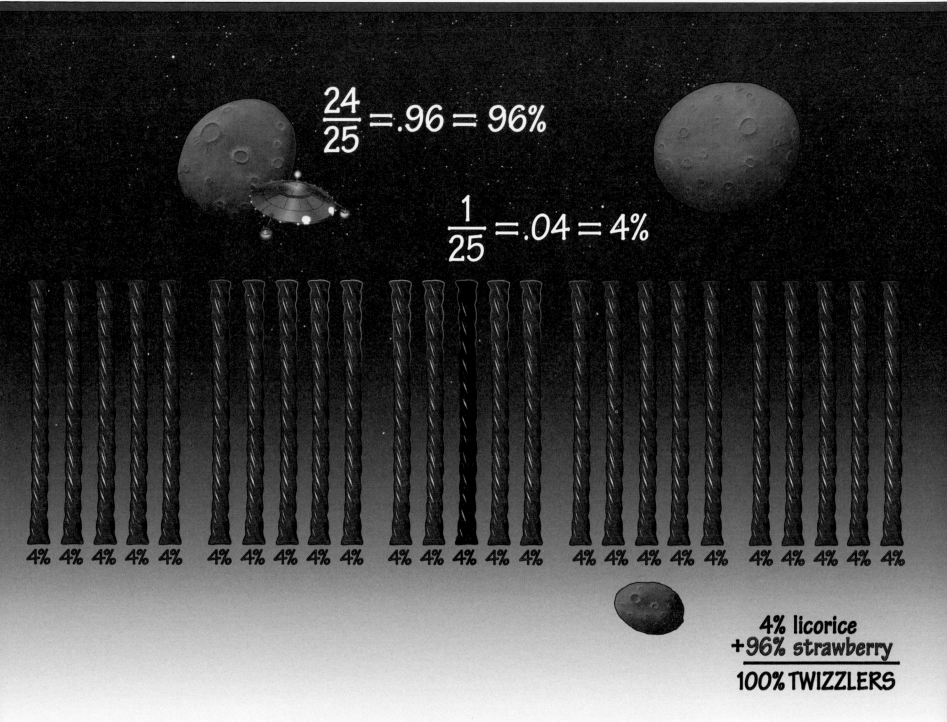

$$\frac{24}{25} = .96 = 96\%$$

$$\frac{1}{25} = .04 = 4\%$$

4% 4% 4% 4% 4%   4% 4% 4% 4% 4%   4% 4% 4% 4% 4%   4% 4% 4% 4% 4%   4% 4% 4% 4% 4%

4% licorice
+96% strawberry
100% TWIZZLERS

In another area, there are twenty-five Twists.
Twenty-four are strawberry-flavored and one is licorice-flavored.
What percent of the total is each piece of candy? Think about it and do the math.

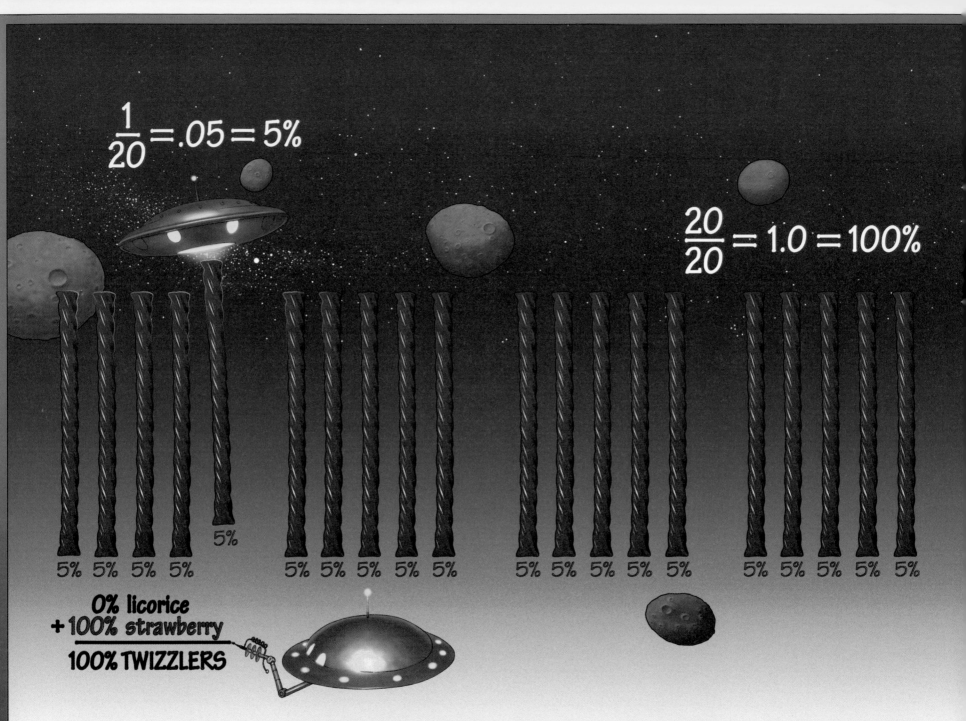

$$\frac{1}{20} = .05 = 5\%$$

$$\frac{20}{20} = 1.0 = 100\%$$

5%

5% 5% 5% 5%   5% 5% 5% 5% 5%   5% 5% 5% 5% 5%   5% 5% 5% 5% 5%

$$\begin{array}{r} 0\% \text{ licorice} \\ + 100\% \text{ strawberry} \\ \hline 100\% \text{ TWIZZLERS} \end{array}$$

If there are twenty TWIZZLERS Twists, each one is five percent of the total. Two would be ten percent, three would be fifteen percent. You can add them if you want to. All of them added together equal one hundred percent, but you know that.

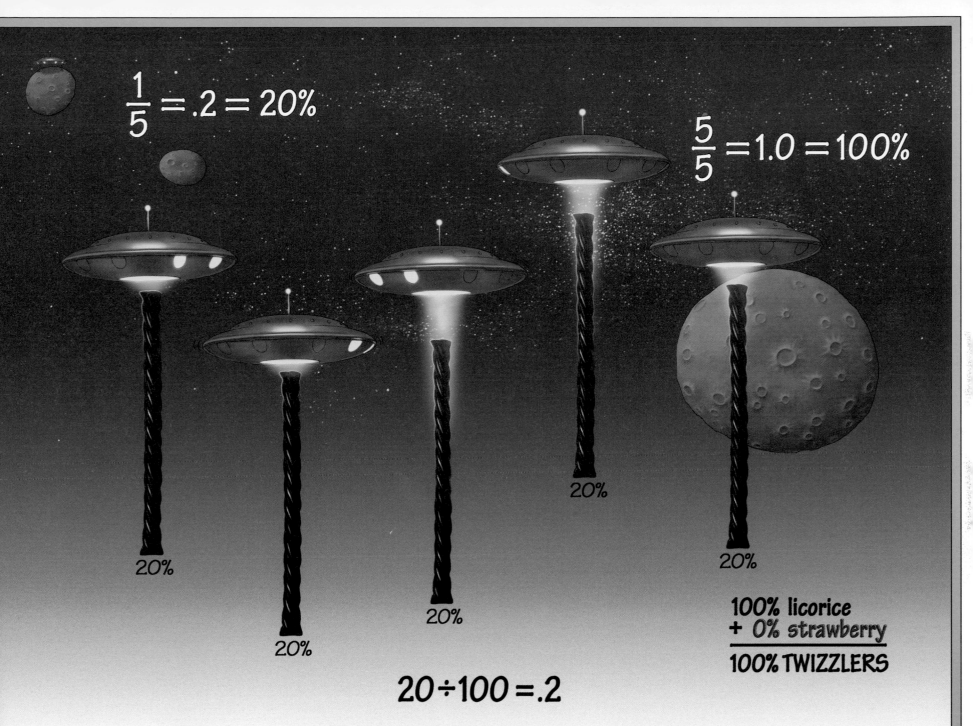

$$\frac{1}{5} = .2 = 20\%$$

$$\frac{5}{5} = 1.0 = 100\%$$

20%

20%

20%

20%

20%

100% licorice
+ 0% strawberry
100% TWIZZLERS

$$20 \div 100 = .2$$

Here we have five Twists. Each Twist is equal to twenty percent. To change a percent to a fraction, drop the percent sign and divide by one hundred. Oops, we are back to a decimal.

AVG	SLG	AB	H	S	2B	3B	HR	BB	OBP
.325	.595	400	130	78	22	4	26	100	.460

.325

A famous Earthling finished the baseball season with a batting average of three-twenty-five! A batting average is a percentage. It is calculated by dividing the number of "hits" by the number of "at bats."

$$H \div AB = AVG$$
$$130 \div 400 = .325$$

.595

The SLG, or "slugging percentage," is calculated by adding singles
as ones, doubles as twos, triples as threes, and home runs
as fours. This number is divided by the total number of "at bats."

$$78 + 44 + 12 + 104 = 238$$

$$238 \div 400 = .595$$

.460

The OBP, or "on-base percentage," is calculated by adding
walks plus hits divided by walks plus "at bats."

$$BB + H \div BB + AB = OBP$$

$$100 + 130 \div 100 + 400 = .460$$

When watching or playing baseball, you are doing math!

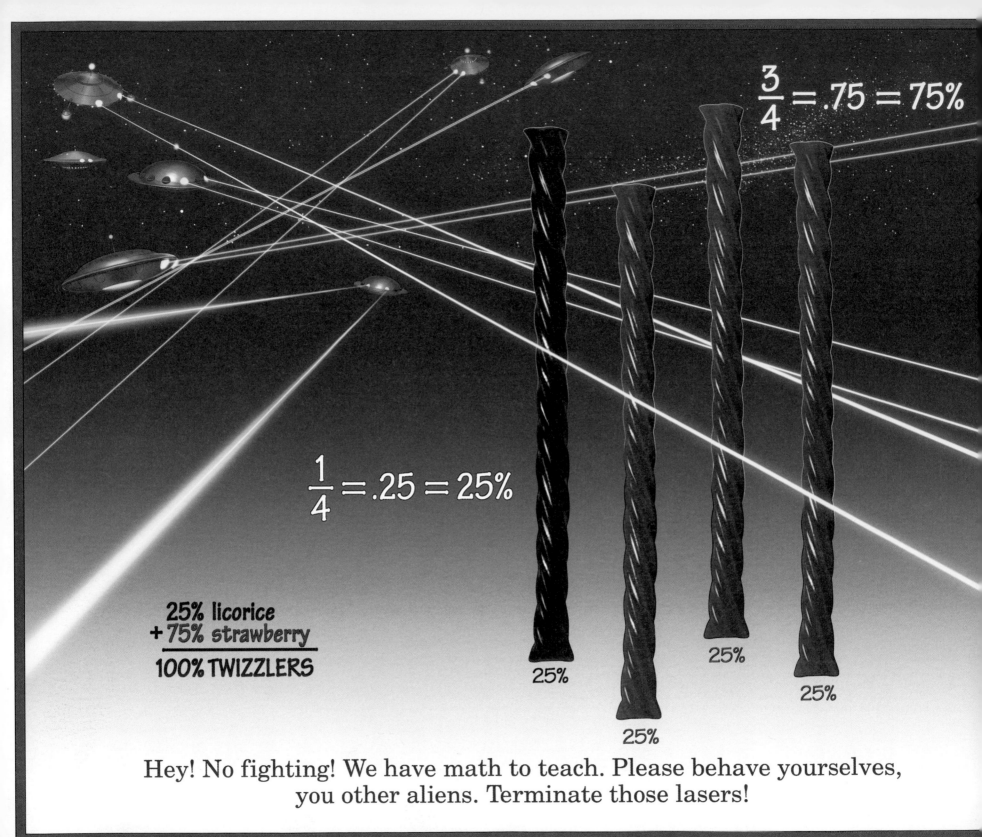

$$\frac{3}{4} = .75 = 75\%$$

$$\frac{1}{4} = .25 = 25\%$$

25% licorice
+ 75% strawberry
—————————
100% TWIZZLERS

25%

25%

25%

25%

Hey! No fighting! We have math to teach. Please behave yourselves,
you other aliens. Terminate those lasers!

$$\frac{2}{3} = .66666666666666666666666666666666666$$

$$\frac{1}{3} = .33333333333333333333333333333333$$

33.333333333

33⅓%

33⅓%

33⅓%

33⅓%

33⅓%

33⅓% licorice
+66⅔% strawberry
100% TWIZZLERS

Not all decimals are easy to understand. Here are three TWIZZLERS Twists. Each one is equal to thirty-three point three three three three three three three three three three three and it keeps going on forever. It is enough to drive you nuts.

Earthlings, there are nine planets in your solar
system. Mercury, Venus, Earth, Mars, Jupiter, Saturn,
Uranus, Neptune, and Pluto. The red strawberry one is our favorite.

$$\frac{1}{9} = .111 = 11.1\% \text{ "Rounded off"}$$

Do you know how many planets in your solar system have life? We are not sure either, but the answer may be one-ninth. One-ninth is equal to eleven point one percent rounded off. We would teach you about "rounding off" non-terminating decimals but it is time for us to go.

There are twenty-five kids in my class. Now that we all know percentages, we can do the math. We each get eight TWIZZLERS Twists. Four percent of the total. Twenty-five percent of the eight are licorice. Seventy-five percent are strawberry. That's it! Two licorice and six strawberry each. That's a ratio of two to six! Our teacher says we will learn about ratios next week. Mini-spaceships, please come back!

homework:
practice my percentages

... no one believes me!

$200 \div 25 = 8$
$\frac{8}{200} = \frac{4}{100} = .04$
4%

2 licorice
6 strawberry

25%

75%

I love percentages!

15 strawberry + 5 licorice = 20 packages	15+5=20
20 packages × 10 pieces = 200 Twizzlers	20×10 = 200
200 Twizzlers ÷ 25 students = 8 pieces each!	200 ÷ 25 = 8

| $\frac{5 \text{ licorice}}{20 \text{ packs}} = \frac{1}{4} = .25 = 25\%$ | $5 \div 5 = 1$ $20 \div 5 = 4$ $= .25 = 25\%$ |
| $\frac{15 \text{ strawberry}}{20 \text{ packs}} = \frac{3}{4} = .75 = 75\%$ | $15 \div 5 = 3$ $20 \div 5 = 4$ $= .75 = 75\%$ |